AF322645

Magical Times

Doing All the Work

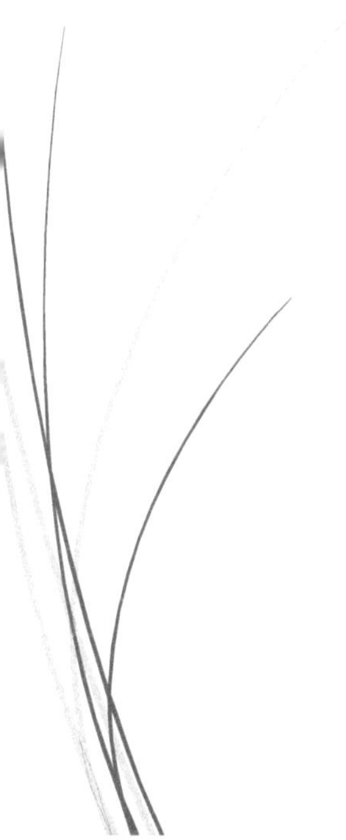

Magical Times #3

Doing All the Work

By AJ Hard

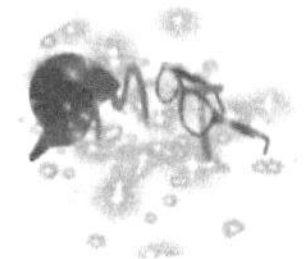

1

Just an Author

Dad spent most of his time in his office. He was working on a new book. He had much time on his hands ever since he was fired from his job.

"How could this happen?" I asked. I lied in bed staring blankly at the ceiling. My twin brother, C.J. was at his desk working on his English homework. He turned back at gazed at me, "A.J., whatever happened Dad doesn't want to talk about it."

I sat up, "But C.J.," I started. "Dad loved that job, what is he going to do without it?"

My brother sighed, "I don't know A.J., coach the tennis team, write books, tutoring." I could tell C.J. spoke in sarcasm. "Dad has a lot going for him. He's not just a teacher."

"I know C.J., but you forget," I started. "Dad loves teaching others. Not to mention that *whole* school loves him."

Steve, our pet dog, came trotting into the bedroom, "Your dad doesn't seem too bummed about it. Meanwhile, it's time for you to master your time-mation spell."

"I thought I did?" I replied. "We used that spell to tell Uncle Anthony about our powers."

Steve was interrupted as a bright flash greeted us. "Hello, boys,"

Great Grandma and her sister, Aunt Willie greeted us.

"Hi Grandma, hi Aunt Willie," we said.

"A.J. you haven't completely mastered the time-mation spell." Grandma Wilma explained. She released a shy smile avoiding eye contact with me.

"But how is that possible? I used the spell. I know I did!" I glued my eyes on my brother, "C.J. back me up here." I said.

"You've minor the future spell, but not the past." Steve explained, "You have to complete both to pass the spell."

I groaned and flopped back onto my bed. "This is terrible!" I groaned.

"How so?" my brother asked. He stood next to me looking down over me.

"Dad got fired from work, I still have a spell to master, and Carson keeps stealing my cereal!" I complained.

"And how is all that terrible?" Great Grandma asked.

"Well, by the time I'm ready to eat, it's nearly..." C.J. cut me off.

"She means about Dad getting fired."

"Oh," I uttered. "I just mean that things aren't going right like they're supposed to."

Suddenly there was a knock at the door. "Come in," we all replied in unison.

It was our cousin Skylar; he was wearing a gamer's muffs. They were like ear muffs, but on his left ear was a mic pressed against his cheek.

He poked his head into our room, "Hold on a sec." he said into the mic. He turned to me, "Uncle Asia wants you two downstairs." he informed.

We nodded in comprehend. Skylar then went back to his video game, "No man, I said hold on. Don't shoot the rocket yet!" He closed the door behind him.

"What do you think he wants?" C.J. wondered. I just shrugged, "I wish you could control your visions." I grumbled as I walked out the door; C.J. followed behind me.

We made our way downstairs and to Dad's room. He was there walking around on his phone.

"Yes, I'll be there." He stated. "I was thinking before lunch, so 10:00?" "Ok, great!" Finally, he hung up the phone. "Hey boys, have a seat."

It was obvious Dad had some exciting news. "Who was that Dad?" C.J. asked. Another school gave you a job?"

We sat on Dad's bed as he sat in his footrest in front of us. "No, but that was your principal."

I didn't like the sound of that. It didn't matter how you say it, the phrase 'that was your principal' doesn't sound good.

C.J. glanced at me from the corner of his eyes, I glared at him back in confusion. I didn't have a clue what he was leading to.

"Boys, I've been asked by your principal to present 'Shiver and Fears' to the school." Dad started. My heart skipped a beat. Don't get me wrong, I was happy for Dad, but Dad being at my school made me feel like I'd swallowed a rock.

Dad continued, "I told her I'd do it only if my boys were ok with it." The room grew silent. Dad was waiting for a response, I was hoping for C.J. say something, I guess he was expecting me to say something.

Finally, C.J. responded, "Well, Dad, I'm ok with it. I mean, most kids at our school love Shiver and Fears books. Madison Yang is *still* telling everyone about *The Headless Robot.*"

"What about you, A.J.?" Dad asked. All eyes were on me. I could feel my heart begin to race, "Yeah Dad, you should totally go for it."

I watched as Dad's smile grew, "Ok then, I'll try not to attract any attention to you guys while I'm there." Dad said.

He picked up his phone and walked out of the room.

"What were you thinking!" I snapped. C.J.'s jaw dropped, "What are you talking about? You said it was ok."

"C.J., if Dad is at our school there's a chance he might be hired to work there," I explained.

"hard, what makes you think Dad wants to work at a middle school?" my brother asked.

I shrugged, "I don't know, but Dad's a good teacher. He'd take a teaching job in a heartbeat."

"A.J., calm down." C.J.requested. "Dad can't work with teenagers, he says their too stiff. He's *not* going to work at our school."

C.J. gladly walked his way out the room. I took a deep breath, I tried to relax. Maybe C.J. was right, Dad wouldn't reunite with his middle school alumni, right? My eyes widen, I bit my lower lip. At least I hope not, I thought.

2

Celebrity at School

Dad was going to be presented in our reading classes, and I was in luck, mine came first.

"It's good to see you again, Ms. Harshaw!" Dad said. He gave her a reuniting hug.

"I'm glad to hear from you after all those years." Ms. Harshaw replied. "What's your latest work?"

Madison tapped me on the shoulder from her seat behind me, "So your dad has been writing for 23 years?"

"Yeah, pretty cool huh?" I said.

Sitting next to me was Holly. She was a very popular 8th grader. Her golden, straight brown hair was tied in a ponytail.

"Anyone can write a story," she stated. "What makes your dad so special?" Ms. Harshaw overheard our conversation, "Well if you must know Holly, after being a student here, he pursued a very difficult task." She began. "Not only did he start a series that everyone loves, but it traveled all over the world, been on several news stations-"

"And I'm working to get the book to become a new tv series!" Dad finished. The whole class murmured in excitement.

"Dad, are you series?" I asked. "Shiver and Fears is becoming a tv show?"

Dad shrugged, "Maybe, it's not official yet."

More murmuring acquired. Dad continued talking to the class about his books, he even read a few chapters. Once the bell rang, Dad packed up all his stuff and made his way to another reading class.

Everyone was overwhelmed with excitement with the thought that Dad's book series would soon be a tv show.

"Hey A.J.," called Robert. "What channel will Shiver and Fears be on?" I was completely speechless. All I did was a shrug of confusion. Dad never told me about Shiver and Fears being a tv show. I started wondering if Dad was just lying to get attention.

"Hey kid, are you August Hardwick?" I turned around. A man wearing a *Channel 4* rain jacket stood behind me.

"Who's asking?" I pondered. I realized he stood next to a man with a camera on his shoulder.

"I'm Blake Hardman," he explained, "from Channel 4 News. We heard the sons of the author AJ Hard go to this school: August and Chadly Hardwick."

I saw an opportunity. I mumbled, "Brother call." Under my breath and snapped my fingers. It was a spell I learned a few years ago. It was made to signal for my brother in times of need.

"Well I'm August, and-" Chadly charged his way around the corner. I gripped his arm and pulled him to my side, "this is my brother Chadly."

"What's going on here?" C.J. questioned.

"Blake Hardman wanted us for some reason," I explained.

"Mind if I take some time out of your class time to interview you two?"

"Really? Oh wow!" I could tell C.J. wanted to jump for joy hearing this.

"Sure, where do you want us?" I asked.

3

No Magic

"A.J., it shouldn't be that hard." Steve declared. Even though he was right, he was wrong. It was hard. I could do this spell where I could present myself in the future and predict it how I wanted to, but I was supposed to be able to do this for the past as well.

Really? What was the point of that? To stop Abe Lincoln's assassination, but not changing *anything* in the future? There's really go good use for that.

"A.J. you can't move on till you complete this," C.J. said.

"I can't do this!" I exclaimed.

"Yes you can, you just-"

"No, I mean I can't do this knowing Dad is spending his Friday morning doing nothing!"

We were all outside: me, C.J., Steve, and Britt. Britt was curious about how long she could do her levitation, C.J. was doing some kind of yoga to clear his mind for his visions, and I had to cast a useless spell.

"What are you three doing out here?" Carson stepped out of her shed-room. She and Granny shared a large shed that was remodeled into a small house.

It was originally made for Granny for the days she planned to visit, but now Carson shares it with her.

"We're practicing Carson, now go away." I snapped.

Carson just retaliated, "I don't have to," she started. "I can be out here just as much as you are." She stood in front of us with her arms crossed.

I was growing impatient with her. "GRANNY!" I called. Granny stepped outside with us, "What's the problem?" she asked.

Granny understood the conflict between Carson and I., And she also knew Carson was always the start of it.

"We're trying to practice, but Carson is in the way," I explained. I knew Granny would shoo her away.

"Steve, you guys can't practice in your bedroom?" Grany asked. My jaw dropped, I wasn't sure I heard correctly.

"Well sure Granny, I can move our lesson upstairs." he was hesitant. Steve was just as shocked as I was.

"I'm sorry Steve, I just...I don't feel comfortable with..." I knew what Granny was trying to say. I knew she loved us, but the thought of magic made her cringe.

"We understand, we'll just go to our room." I led Britt and C.J. inside with Steve by my side.

I didn't see it, but I knew Carson had a smile on her face indicating she won. It was a feeling that boiled inside of me. The feeling didn't stop, As I shut the slide-glass door, I watched as Carson walked back in the shed-room.

"You guys finished practicing outside?" Uncle Brandon asked. He was relaxed on the couch watching a sitcom.

"We're done outside, but we're not done." I hinted. Just as I requested saying that, Uncle Brandon asked what's the matter.

"Carson used Granny to shoo us back inside because she knows Granny hates the fact of magic."

Uncle Brandon chuckled with a huff, "Come sit with me, nephew." Steve and my siblings made their way upstairs as I sat next to my uncle.

"Your Grandma didn't make good choices when she was a kid. When she dedicated her life to Christ, she wanted to be sure God forgave her for her sins."

As he explained this, I could see my great grandma, staying hidden, agreeing with her grandson.

"But God already forgave her, and what does that have to do with our magic, and why does-” Uncle Brandon stopped me.

“Just understand August, magic isn’t always a blessing. I’m not even sure how it’s a blessing myself.”

“Maybe Grandma can explain it better.” I thanked my uncle and made my way upstairs. Grandma followed behind me.

“Is everything ok, A.J.?” she asked. I didn’t answer, because I wasn’t so sure myself. I didn’t say a word till I got to my room and closed the door behind me.

4

The Truth

The next day was Saturday. I woke up with the mood to do nothing. Dad was coaching at tennis practice, Britt was at Elsy B dance practice, and C.J. was a tennis game.

The house was mostly empty. The only person here was Skylar and Granny.

"What's the problem, youngling?" Great Aunt Willie was shining in golden lighting from the window. She fluttered her wings as she placed her feet on the floor.

I sat up in bed, "I know you gave up the powers because we're the family twins, but why magic? Isn't it frowned upon for Christians?"

Great Aunt smiled, "You're right, giving you powers of dark magic is a big no to the heavens," I began to slump.

I felt the soft touch of my great aunt's hand lift my chin, her warm smile approached my face. She explained in a soft tone, "but not only are not the ones who gave you the power, but your powers *aren't* magic."

I was utterly baffled, "What do you mean?" All she did was a wink.

"Time will soon come, but for now let's practice that spell so we can solve that problem that's bothering you."

I smile spread across my face. I jumped off the bed and took a deep breath, "So what good will this spell do?"

"The future spell will help show you your options when making a choice," Great Aunt explained. "But when being presented the past, you'll get answers to the question you ask."

I closed my eyes and took a moment to concentrate "Vision time in the past!" I pointed my left hand outward, and in no time I was at Dad's teaching job.

I hadn't been at Rising Academy before over the summer. It was a small school with many rooms. I was standing in the middle of a hallway. I heard multiple voices from every direction, but one direction sounded the most familiar.

It was Dad, he was talking to someone, and the conversation was happening behind me. I slowly made my way toward the principal's office. Though the window I saw Dad. He was there conversating with Principal Shonda. From the looks of it, things weren't going well.

One thing that caught my attention was Principal Shonda was facing my direction but didn't notice me.

"Step in," Great Aunt Willie surprised me from behind.

"What?" I asked.

"Step in," she repeated.

"I can't just walk into a private conversation.' I whispered. Great Aunt smiled started shoving me toward the door. I thought she was going to press me against the door, but instead, I went right through it.

Dad was seated in an office chair, and he seemed upset. "But Ms. Shonda, why does it matter?" he snapped. "Not to mention all the other stuff these kids get away with-"

"Mr. Asia, are you telling me you'd rather believe your daughter over the 12 kids who all say they saw her climb the slide." The principal replied.

"No one said anything about Jan or Tri climbing the slide."

"Mr. Asia, you need to stop letting your favorites-"

"I DON'T HAVE FAVORITES!" Dad testified. H took a moment to calm down, "Ms. Shonda, I think my daughter and I need some time off. It's obvious she's not happy here, and I just need time to find her another school."

Dad didn't say another word, neither did his boss. He got out of his seat and walked out the door.

5

Britt's School

Things were a little different waking up in the morning. Britt was up and eating breakfast before I could even brush my teeth. A yawn escaped my lips as I stumbled into the kitchen.

Britt sat at the table gulping down a bowl of Lucky Charms. "What's got you so bright eyed and bushy tailed?" A phrase Dad used a lot.

"I'm so excited, I'm going to Britton Elementary today," Britt replied, swallowing a spoonful of cereal.

"Has anyone seen-" Dad strolled in and was just as surprised as I was seeing Britt all dressed and ready for school.

"Hi Dad," she cheered.

"Britt, I'm not quite sure I'm ok with you going to this school," Dad explained. "You might struggle with being in a bigger school."

"Dad, there's nothing to worry about," Britt said. "I'll be fine." Britt seemed for sure, but Dad obviously wasn't.

"Meanwhile, you need to get ready as well A.J." Dad glared at me as I stood in my pajamas.

I slumped my way back to my room, "No need to worried," I yawned. "I'll be ready in a minu-second."

"I'm sorry I taught you that," Dad complained.

"Dad, what exactly *is* a minu-second?" Britt asked.

Dad explained to her what it was; the truth is, I didn't know either. But it was something Dad said a lot.

"You won't believe where Britt is," I said to C.J. as I walked in the door.

"In the bathtub?" he answered. C.J. was getting dressed wearing a green sweater vest over a white shirt.

"No, she's in the kitchen eating cereal."

"Wow, she must really be excited about her new school." C.J. said, "I can't believe Dad got so mad he pulled Britt out of Rising Acadamy."

That when I remembered, "C.J., that reminds me," I started. "Dad didn't get fired, he quit!" C.J. stared at me with confusion, "What do you mean?"

"That past spell I learned, I traveled to Dad's job and saw Dad." I gripped my brother by the shoulders. "Dad walked out on the job."

"Are you sure?" C.J. asked. " You know you tend to over think things." C.J. had a point, I've learned to listen to him a little more over time. "Why would Dad walk out on his teaching job?"

I glared around, there was no one in the dining room. I leaned over to my brother and whispered in his ear, "I think Britt-"

"Kids, it's time to get going," Mom called. "Let's go, let's go!" We scrambled our stuff and made our way "Dad, what about you?" C.J. asked, heading out the door.

He was in the corner of the living room gluing his eyes to his computer screen, "I'll be fine kids," he started. "I have a tennis lesson to prepare for. C.J., don't forget your racket." C.J nodded and followed everyone else to the car.

Britt was bouncing for joy as she sat in between my brother and me.

"Britt, calm down," I commanded. "It's not that serious. You're going to school, not the carnival."

Britt combed her hair, with her fingers, behind her ears. She had a huge grin glued on her face.

"This school must be *really* great," C.J. said rolling his eyes. He was about to say something else when he froze.

"Is your brother having a vision?" Mom asked as she continued her eyes on the road.

"Yes, Mom," Britt answered.

"A.J., get your brother's notebook out his backpack."

I dug through C.J.'s stuff and found a small green notebook, I pulled it out and grabbed a pencil as well. C.J. closed his eyes and shook his head.

"You got my book?" C.J. asked. I handed it to him.

"What did you see?" Britt asked. Before he could give an answer, Mom stopped at a tall building.

"Here we are, Brighton Elementary School," announced Mom.

Britt began exiting the car, "The best part is, Dad has no record at this school." she swung her bag on her back and shut the door.

"What is your sister talking about?" Mom asked. Glaring at us through the mirror.

"C.J. and I are labeled as 'descendants of Asia Hardwick,'" I explained. "So we have expectations from the teachers."

Mom was starting to get concerned, "Do I need to have a word with the teachers?"

"No Mom, we're cool with it. It's not that serious" C.J. closed his notebook and placed it back in his backpack.

"Yeah, we're used to it. It doesn't bother us." I explained. Mom accepted it, but she wasn't so sure as she drove us to our school.

6

The Neighbor Awaits

This was a disaster, and there was no one to blame for it but me. At school, Ian planted a love note in my locker. And like a fool I fell for it.

I could still feel the rage as I watch Ian and his stupid friends laughing and pointing. Something came over me at that point, I could have used my time spell and worked out the outcome, or even the spell I learned in 3rd grade where I can hear the thoughts of others.

I had a whole list of ideas of how to avoid this problem, but I didn't think about them till now. The best way to solve my issue at that point was to kick him.

Not only did I kick him, but Ian also bent over in pain, and I slapped him across the face then knocked him over. My actions caused a load of attention in the hallway. And one person that caught the most attention was a science teacher; Ms. Cutbirth.

This led to a parent-teacher conference, which led to Mom setting up a... play date. The thought made my stomach flip.

What was worse was because of me, C.J. was in this too. We both stood in our front yard, staring at the house right across from us.

Dad was not ok with this, and I agree with him. How Mom was able to convince this to happen, I will never know.

"We have to go, A.J.," my brother said. I gulped and felt a rock go down my throat. I know my brother was regretting this too.

The truth was, there was a part of me that was afraid of Ian. Sure, he was pretty dim but as tough as I seem I actually don't do conflict: which was Ian's favorite thing.

We walked slowly toward our doom across the street. C.J. was more nervous than I was. He took deep breathes loudly, "C.J. calm down." I ordered.

"I don't like this," he replied. "Ian doesn't want to be friends with us."

"Maybe if we're nice to him, he'll be nice to us," I suggested. C.J. wasn't buying it. I gave a shrug.

"A.J., he NEVER liked us." My brother sighed. I huffed and suggested an idea. "Maybe there's something we can do,"

It didn't take long for my brother to know what I was thinking. He nodded his head and led me to the left side of the Alexanders' house where no one could see us, "Vision time in the future!"

We stood inside Ian's house, "And don't mess us anything!" Ian's dad snapped. I felt a chill down my back.

"Y-yes, sir." I stuttered. He disappeared into another room. The house was... lived in. It was as though the furniture was from a garage sale, and the Alexander family let themselves go- or something.

Ian sat on the couch, eyes glued to the tv, playing a video game. "What do you losers want?" he asked.

C.J. and I glared at each other with worried looks. Finally, I responded, "I-I wanted to say- I shouldn't have- hit you."

Ian paused his game and narrowed his eyes at us, "It's ok," he stood us and approached us. "I guess I did deserve it."

They were words of gratitude, but for some reason, I wasn't convinced.

"No, it was wrong of my brother to punch you," Ian shoved my brother to the side, "Shut-up!" he commanded.

I started to back up, "Ian, c-calm down." I stuttered some more, "let's just bury the hatchet a-a-and make anew."

"Good idea," Ian said. "Let's start with the burying!" Ian raised his fist and got ready to knock me out.

7

Ok Friend-enemies

I opened my eyes, C.J. and I were back outside. "W-what happened?" I asked.

"I don't know," C.J. said. "You let go of my hand, but we were still in the future. How did we end up outside?"

I shrugged my shoulders, "I don't know, but I don't want to try it again. I need to test that spell before calling it complete."

"Should we go to Ian's house?"

"I don't want to, but we have to; Principal's orders and Mom's idea," I explained.

C.J. sighed, "Ok, but don't say ANYTHING about punching him."

We walked to the door and knocked. In just a few seconds a tall man answered the door. It was Mr. Alexander, he was not only tall but chunky too. He had black hair that was balding, most of his hair was on his face. A thick mustache went around his lips and gathered under his chin.

His bushy, dark beard had a few grey hairs. What made me want to gag was the hair poking out of his nose. "What do you punks want?" I gave a nervous smile. I tried to focus on his eyes, but instead, I gazed at the concrete porch.

"We're here to hang with Ian."

"I don't allow Hardwicks in my house." Mr. Alexander was about the slam to the door in our face,

"Wait, Mr. Alexander!" C.J. called. " We were ordered from our school principal to schedule a play-date. If we don't, then we'll all be in a pickle."

Mr. Alexander huffed and opened back the door. C.J. and I walked inside. "You're not welcomed long, so don't get comfortable." Ian's dad grumbled. "And don't mess us anything!" those words still send a chill down my back.

Ian stared blankly at the video game he was playing. I was too nervous to say something, I waited for my brother to start a conversation.

"Mind if we play?" C.J. asked. Ian said nothing. C.J. repeated, "Mind if we-"

"Buzz off!" he sneered.

I was going to risk my life for this, but I had to say something, "I never understood why you've come to hate us. We've never done anything to you."

Ian paused his game and stood up. I was in defense mode. I balled my hands into fists as Ian approached me. C.J.'s eyes widened as he placed his hands on my shoulders.

"Your dad never told you what happened?"

My brother and I exchanged glances, and both turned to Ian; we both shook our heads in confusion.

Ian motioned for us to come closer, he whispered to us, "Your dad humiliated my dad." Our eyes widened. "What?" I choked. "What do you mean?"

"Dad's one of the kindest people I know," C.J. responded. "What happened?" Ian shrugged and shook his head.

C.J. and I were both surprised by this information. There was something about Dad we never knew. That is if Ian was truthful. Which, maybe he wasn't.

"Listen, I don't know much about the rivalry between our families,' Ian explained, but maybe we can find out."

"You mean- as friends?" I asked in amazement.

Ian rolled his eyes, "No. Look, we don't have to be friends, we just need to call a truce." Ian held out his hand. I wasn't quite sure what he was doing, C.J. did. He gripped his hand and gave him a handshake. I did the same.

"Now I suggest you get out of my house." He jeered.

I sneered as my brother, and I walked out the door.

"C.J., do you really think Dad really bulled Mr. Alexander?" I asked.

"I don't know, but there's one way to find out,"

"Ask him?" I suggested.

"No, A.J. You have to master that time spell, and we need to see Dad and Mr. Alexander's past."

As I thought about it, I realized C.J. was starting to sound like me. My brother isn't really the snoop into people's business and problems. One thing he was into though, was a good mystery. And this mystery was *so* big; it actually interested *three* people.

8

Past Future Visions

C.J. sat on his bed with his book in front of him. His eyes were closed, it was like looking at a yoga instructor.

Earlier, he revisited his visions. He was trying to do it again. "So when are we going to the pool party?" I asked.

"Shh! I'm trying to concentrate!" he snapped.

I was at my desk collecting notes of The Dust Bowl- totally boring.

"Good job C.J., if you keep picturing your visions your mind will control them and return." assured our pet dog. He trotted over to me and hopped on my lap, "Why aren't you working on your time spells?"

I groaned. "I have homework to do, and until I get a 'finishing homework' spell, I have to do it myself.

"Even if you had a spell to do homework, you should still do the homework yourself." A bright light flashed beside me, and my great aunt made an appearance.

"Hi Great Aunt Willie, listen about the time spell-"

"Don't worry, A.J. School work is more important than your training. I actually came by to let you know something." She explained.

It got all three of our attention. "You need to be more thoughtful with your spells." Aunt Willie pointed at me.

"What? What do you mean?" I asked, "I can choose whatever spell I want, right?"

"Yes A.J.," Steve started. "But understand, you weren't given these powers just because you're a twin, you were given them to help others." I was very confused about what everyone was telling me.

"I have been, haven't I?"

"A.J., you used your teleportation spell to take Ian's pants," C.J. revealed.

"No to mention, you used it to put a spider in his mouth!" Aunt Willie added.

"But I did that to help another kid at school from being blamed for a food fight." Everyone gave me a stern look, even Steve.

I sighed, "Ok, ok I'll be more aware of my spells."

C.J. was about to say something else when he froze in place, it wasn't long though. Within ¾ of a minute, he returned.

"What did you see?" I asked. C.J. didn't answer. Instead, he wrote in his notebook with confusion on his face.

"Was it about the pool party?" I asked. He still didn't answer.

"Is there something wrong, C.J.?" Aunt Willie asked. C.J. closed his book and began to give some answers.

"Yeah, but something didn't make sense." He started, "it was Dad, he was at our school with Mr. Alexander. They were... laughing together."

"Wow, that really *doesn't* make sense," said Steve.

"That's not it, what didn't make sense was Dad and Mr. Alexander looked like kids!" C.J.'s eyes widened, "I think I saw the past. Can I do that?"

"No, you can only see the future, seeing the past too is way too advanced," Steve explained.

"So wait, so what I'm hearing is, it is possible," I stated. No one said anything. "Well, C.J. is smart. Who's to say he didn't advance into it?"

"A.J., magic isn't like school. You have to take your time in it," explained Aunt Willie.

"So what did I see?" my brother baffled.

"Are you sure it was Dad and Mr. Alexander? I mean, you said they were laughing together."

"A.J., Mr. Alexander looked a little different, but I can recognize our own father."

"Chill out bro, I'm trying to help figure this out." C.J. seemed concerned.

"It seems to me there's something on your minds that need an answer," Aunt Willie said.

"Well visions sometimes come from thoughts and questions," Steve explained. "Maybe the vision is an answer to a question or thought you have?"

My head started to spin. I never really knew there was so much detail to having visions. Past visions? Thoughts? Questions? All I had to do was... Then it came to me.

I jumped out of my seat, "I'm going to practice my time animation spells." I snatched my brother's hand and motioned my other, "Vision time in the past!"

9

Dad's Best Friend

We were placed in our school, but things looked a little different. I suddenly realized we were n 8th Grade Hall.

"What have you done?" C.J. asked. He released my hand, and once again, we didn't travel back. "Are we stuck in this time?"

I shrugged my shoulders, "I hope not, but we still need to solve this mystery." I explained.

"What mystery? Where are we? What have you done!"

"Chill out C.J," I commanded. C.J. was intense, but I knew this would give us answers to our question. It might even get a truce between Ian and our parents.

We heard the bell ring and students began walking out of the classrooms. "Where were you, when you had the vision?" I asked my brother.

"I-I don't know, there was a case of stairs in the background. So somewhere up here."

I grabbed C.J.'s hand, and we made our way quickly toward the stairs. In no time we saw Dad and Mr. Alexander. Just like my brother predicted, they were side by side laughing.

"They look like friends," I examined. "They're more bonded then than they are now."

"Ian said Dad bullied Mr. Alexander," C.J. said, "but Dad's not that kind of person."

"Good point, let's follow them." We traveled the halls as the two boys led us to a classroom.

Dad and his friend sat next to each other in the middle row.

"Where do we go?" C.J. asked.

"Shhh," I commanded.

"Can they hear us?"

"I don't know, but still keep quiet!" We both sat quietly in between the two boys. As the teacher began talking, I watched Dad as he leaned over and whispered to Ian's dad.

"What are you doing Friday?"

Mr.Alexander rolled his eyes and whispered back, "I'm grounded for the next two weeks, no company."

"Gosh, this is boring." With just a thought in my head, I sent us back home.

"Wait, wait?!" C.J. cried. We were back in our bedroom. C.J. gave me a hard punch, "Why did you do that?"

"What was the point? There wasn't anything there."

Wait, where did you kids go?" Steve asked. He and Aunt Willie still stood in front of us.

"A.J. took me to Dad's past, turns out he was friends with Ian's dad."

"But, it all doesn't make sense." I started, "Ian said Dad bullied Mr. Alexander. Aunt Willie, do you know anything about this?"

She glared at us with grace, "I do know the story, but an angel is not to tell of someone's past."

"So Our only answer is to ask Dad himself," C.J. replied.

I crossed my arms and huffed. "Dad will NEVER tell us about his friendship with Mr. Alexander." I could remember the narrow glare he gets when even saying the name Alexander. It was almost similar to the name Sheffield (whoever they are.)

"It won't hurt to ask," Aunt Willie explained. She then made an exit with a big, bright ball of light.

"Won't hurt to ask?" I repeated, "Dad will be furious if he knows what we did."

"She does have a point, boys," Steve said. "If your dad is willing to explain about hos friendship will the neighbors, that's his choice."

I could tell I was cornered, there was no fighting it. C.J. and I made our way downstairs.

We walked into the living room where Dad usually spends his time before writing, but he wasn't there. Instead, Uncle Brandon was there relaxed on the couch.

"Uncle Brandon, have you seen Dad?" I asked.

He pointed outside, "He's on the phone with an important call." I figured C.J. wouldn't want to bother him. If it was an important call, my brother knew not to interrupt. I was wrong.

He pulled the glass door and saw Dad pacing around talking to someone with amazement.

"Yes, I can start bright and early Monday morning." "yes, and thank you!"

"Dad, can I ask you something?" C.J. asked. From the worried looks on our faces, Dad knew this was serious.

"As serious as it seems, I have great news. That was Britton Elementary,"

"and they want you to make an appearance at the school?" I said.

"Wel sort of," Dad started. "They want me to be a teacher at the school, and help with the library."

"Dad, does this mean what I think it does?" C.J. asked.

"It means Dad going to be an amazing teacher once again!" The three of us began dancing around the yard.

Carson stepped out Granny's yard house "What's going on out here?" she asked.

"Dad is working as a teacher again!" I cheered. Carson shrugged, "Cool." And walked back inside.

We were all happy, but the excitement was cut short when Dad said, "Now what is it you want to ask me?"

10

Story with No Ending

"Why would you kids do such a thing?" Dad asked with displeasure. C.J. and I both hung our heads low.

We were all in the living room: me, C.J., Dad, Mom, Aunt Cameo, Uncle Brandon, Skylar, Carson, Steve... Yes, everyone was there.

"A.J., how could you so reckless with your powers!" Granny snapped. "Snooping on your father's past is like reading someone's diary." I felt so ashamed, I didn't dare look up to see everyone staring at us; they were like beams of heat burning holes on my body.

"I just don't understand, what caused you two to do this?" Dad asked. "Why am *I* your target in this whole thing?"

Even though I had an answer, I didn't know what to say. C.J. was speechless too.

"I would think *you'd* know better, C.J." Mom scolded.

"But Mom, we were just trying to help," C.J. explained.

"How is snooping on your father helping?" Aunt Cameo sneered.

"Dad, you're a great teacher," I answered. "We just wanted to know why you weren't interested in getting your job back."

"And what about snooping through his childhood?" Skylar asked.

"I told you," I started turning toward Dad, "Ian's dad blamed you for whatever happened in middle school."

Dad sighed, "Guys, that's *my* business. You have no need to be involved in it."

Skylar tapped him on the shoulder, "Well Uncle, maybe you should explain. What is the deal between you and the Alexander family?"

All eyes were on our father. "Ok, ok. I'll explain" he caved in. "The thing about it is, I don't know what happened." No one seemed to understand.

"So you didn't bully him?" Carson asked.

"If I did, I never knew. All I remember was asking Isaac to come over my house, and he told me I was a jerk."

"Well Asia, maybe instead of bickering and fighting you should talk to him," Granny suggested.

"Mom, he wouldn't listen then, and he won't listen now!"

The whole family began to discuss issues between the Hardwicks and the Alexanders.

Uncle Brandon pulled my brother and I out of it, "Listen you two, you both have powers that are supernatural, but make sure you're using them for the right reasons, understand?" C.J. and I nodded in unison.

Uncle Brandon walked back into the living room with everyone else.

"C.J. we got to go to our room." I led the way to our bedroom upstairs.

I shut the door behind us and locked it.

"C.J., none of this makes sense: is or isn't Dad's the fault?" I pressed my back against the door.

"I don't know, if Dad *did* do something it wasn't obvious."

My brother was making just as much sense as the whole feud. "What do you mean?"

"If Dad *did* bully Mr. Alexander, he didn't have a clue about it. Not to mention, Dad wasn't trying to."

"I guess our only decision is to visi-"

"Don't you dare!" called a voice from the heaven. From a ball of light appeared Great Grandma... or Great

Aunt Willie. I actually couldn't tell at this time.

"Now A.J. and C.J. your whole family just had a word with you about magical snooping."

C.J. called me out, "That wasn't me, that's him!" he said pointing at me. I narrowed my eyes at him.

"Sorry, I guess I forgot," I replied.

"Boys, before you start moving on to your next lesson, put your mission on hold, and start thinking about how these miracles can help others."

"Yes, Granny Wilma." C.J. agreed.

"Wait, did you say miracles?" I asked. "And you're Granny Wilma?"

"I'm sending my husband down to Earth to secure you with responsibility for a while," she said.

My jaw dropped, "What?!"

Great Grandma said nothing more, she changed into a ball of light and faded away.

"See what your actions did?" C.J. snapped.

"What? You're the one who had the vision!" I replied.

"You just *had* to mess with Ian and get us in this mess."

We stopped arguing when we heard a knock at the door, "Boys, it's me, Britt. Open the door."

I unlocked the door, and Britt just barged in, "This is terrible! Dad's working at *my* school again."

"I thought you just wanted a new school?" C.J. asked.

"I wanted a new school *away* from Dad." she pouted as she plopped on my bed.

I moped at C.J. and sighed, "Looks like we all have an issue to look forward to."

The three of us sat in the room; all of us moped. It seemed life was not getting any easier. Not to mention, the feud was a bigger mystery than we thought.

THE STORY BEHIND THE STORY

A.J., Britt, and C.J. are worried about their dad now that he's not a teacher anymore. But their dad uses his writing career as a reason not to worry about it.

Meanwhile, A.J. has gotten into a situation with Ian and have to make amends with his neighbor. This causes the brothers to realize there is a missing puzzle piece that might solve the issue between their father and Ian's.

WHAT HAPPENS NEXT

A.J. and C.J. must learn how to use their powers to help others. A.J. must figure out his next move that Grandpap Leslie will approve of. Can he find a spell that can do that? Find out in the new book Magical Times: That Won't Work